Grow Your Own Bean Plant!

Contents

How to Grow a Bean Plant	2
Getting Started	4
Shoots and Roots	6
Leaves and Stem	8
Planting	10
Pods	12
Harvesting the Beans	14
Index	16

Joseph Ciciano

How to Grow a Bean Plant

This book will show you how to grow your own bean plant. All plants need food, light and water in order to grow. To grow your own bean plant you will need a few more things!

Getting Started

First, fold a paper towel into a tube.
Place the paper tube inside a glass jar.
Next, fill the jar with water.

Then put two or three bean seeds between the paper tube and the glass sides of the jar.

Shoots and Roots

After seven days, check what has happened to the seeds. You should now be able to see a shoot growing from the top of the seed.

You should also be able to see a root growing downwards.
Keep the jar in a light place.

Leaves and Stems

After two weeks, the bean plant should be much bigger. By now it should have a long stem and leaves.

You should also be able to see the roots beginning to fill the glass jar.

Planting

By now your bean plant should have tiny white flowers. Soon, pods will grow from these. It is time to put the bean plant into a pot. First use the trowel to fill a pot with compost.

flowers

Make a hollow in the compost and carefully put the roots of the plant into it. Cover the roots with compost, and keep moist by watering the plant.

Pods

pod

cane

A cane will support the plant as it grows.

The plant has taken the food it needs to grow from the compost.

Pods should now be growing on the bean plant. When the pods are about 10 centimetres long they are ready to be picked.

Harvesting the Beans

Pinch the pods carefully off the stems of the plant. Gently open the pods. You will see all the beans inside.

Pull the beans out of the pod. Now they are ready to be cooked and eaten!

Index

bean seeds 2, 5, 6

cane 3, 12

compost 2, 10-11, 12

flowers 10-11

leaves 8-9

light 2, 7

pods 10, 12-13, 14

root 7, 9, 11

shoot 6-7

stem 8-9

tube 4-5

water 2, 4